SUMMARY
of Thomas L. Friedman's
THANK YOU FOR BEING LATE

An Optimist's Guide to Thriving in the Age of Accelerations

by SUMOREADS

TABLE OF CONTENTS

Key Takeaway: The age of average, high-paid middle-skilled jobs, is over.

Key Takeaway: The age of accelerations is ushering in a workplace that demands new social contracts.

Key Takeaway: Accelerations in the three forces are stressing states, threatening geopolitical stability

Key Takeaway: Social media offers freedom from, not freedom to.

Key Takeaway: Technology empowers breakers as much as it empowers makers.

Key Takeaway: The ability to adapt determines the states and cultures that survive in the age of accelerations.

Key Takeaway: Technological innovation must be accompanied by moral innovation.

Key Takeaway: A healthy community is the bedrock of socio-economic prosperity.

Key Takeaway: Healthy communities are built on collaboration and compromise.

Key Takeaway: Navigating the age of accelerations takes inclusion and adaptation.

EXECUTIVE SUMMARY

In his book *Thank You for Being Late: An Optimist's Guide to Thriving in the Age of Accelerations*, Thomas L. Friedman explores the three forces driving the global economy and explains how individuals, institutions, and governments can leverage these forces and cushion their adverse effects.

Friedman contends that simultaneous accelerations in technology, globalization, and climate change are fueling what he calls "the Machine" and changing virtually every aspect of modern life. Rapid advances in technology are making it easier, faster, and cheaper for more people to connect and collaborate; globalization is making more countries dependent and more industries obsolete; and climate change is driving economic and political unrest and threatening the planetary systems that sustain life.

In Friedman's view, these accelerating changes are only unsettling because people are not learning and adapting fast enough to catch up with the global flows shaping the world. Progress—Friedman argues—no longer hinges on a left or right political system, or on possession of vast resources; it hinges on openness to global flows. Individuals, business, and governments that thrive in the age of accelerations will be the ones who continuously seek out and embrace new ideas, diversity, and pluralism.

Friedman goes in search of the people influencing the three forces to help the reader make sense of the future of business, community, and government. Towards the end, he takes the reader to his hometown of St. Louis Park, Minnesota, to illustrate the kind of inclusive community that fosters trust, learning, pluralism, and common-good politics and, consequently, flourishes in the age of accelerations.

PART I:
REFLECTING

Key Takeaway: Pause and reflect to make sense of accelerating change.

Three major forces in the world today—globalization, technology, and climate change—are accelerating simultaneously and at an overwhelming pace, changing much of what it means to work, do business, interact, and live.

Anyone who wishes to understand and, consequently, be on the right side of these forces, has to pause and reexamine his beliefs, his assumptions, and his understanding of what is possible. All the change, knowledge, and connection in the world today is only meaningful if you can pause and reflect on it.

Today, it's easier to be a part of history—to influence people and policies—than it has ever been. But you can only influence people if you have a solid value set, if you understand how the forces that move the world work, and if you understand how these forces affect people and cultures.

To thrive in the age of accelerations, you have to keep learning and acquiring and combining perspectives. You can't understand or explain the world if you keep thinking within or outside the box. You must overlook the box and search beyond the disciplines that affect or interest you.

PART II:
ACCELERATING

Key Takeaway: The age of accelerations is ushering in uncomfortable changes.

If there ever was an inflection point in technology, 2007 was it: Steve Jobs launched the iPhone, Facebook and Twitter began marching to global domination, Google launched Android, the number of Internet users crossed the one billion mark, Palantir Technologies launched its big data analytics platform, and the clean power revolution began.

These technologies became a reality because the prediction made by Moore's law—that computational processing power would double about every two years—had been holding true for about five decades. The technologies being launched today are still within the first half of the exponential growth curve expected to follow Moore's law.

Globalization and climate change are on a similar trajectory. Their rate of change and the acceleration of this change is as dramatic as that of technology. Commercially and socially, the world is getting hyper-connected and hyper-dependent. The global population is exploding, and biodiversity is getting decimated.

The three forces are interacting and driving even more accelerated change. They are not just disrupting the world; they are dislocating entire societies and institutions.

Key Takeaway: Individuals and societal structures are falling behind the rate of technological change.

In the early 20th century, it took about twenty to thirty years for major technological innovations such as the airplane to make a significant impact in the world. Before that, entire centuries could go virtually unchanged. Today, with technologies rapidly building off previous technologies, it takes about six years for a new technology to spread around the globe and throw the entire world off balance. Although individuals and societies are adapting to these changes faster than they did in the past, the rate of adaptation—including the rate at which laws to regulate these technologies are made—is beginning to fall behind the rate of technological change.

"The rate of technological change is now accelerating so fast that it has risen above the average rate at which most people can absorb all these changes. Many of us cannot keep pace anymore" (Kindle Locations 481-482).

The immediate solution is faster and lifelong learning. Society has to increase its adaptability by rethinking its institutions, experimenting with speed, and continually reevaluating its regulations. In part, being adaptable means developing new school curriculums every few years.

Key Takeaway: Computational power is increasing at an exponential rate.

When the U.S government launched the ASCI Red in 1997, it was the most advanced computer of its time. It processed 1.8 teraflops—1.8 trillion floating-point calculations per second—

, cost $55 million to make, occupied space the size of a tennis court, and required electricity that could power eight hundred houses. By 2006, Sony had made and was mass-selling a tiny device with as much computational for a fraction of the price—the PlayStation 3.

Today, Intel is developing a fingernail-sized microchip that fits over one billion transistors (tiny switches, the speed of which determines computational power). This development will be a gigantic leap from its bulky 1970s transistors that had just a few thousand transistors. Computers—as Gordon Moore predicted in the 1960s—are getting faster, cheaper, smaller, and more efficient at an exponential rate.

Key Takeaway: Sensors and big data are doing away with guessing.

Increasing computational power has enabled the development of sensors that capture image, sound, temperature, pressure, and movement and ushered in the age of "predictive maintenance." Modern garbage cans and fire hydrants, for example, have sensors that alert maintenance crews when they are full or when pressure is too high. Just a few years ago, it took career-long experience to detect subtle inefficiencies and make early adjustments. Today, sensors are amplifying weak signals and giving workers instant information to make accurate predictions, optimize operations, and save costs.

When Google described a way to link thousands of computer drives and store and search a mountain of data in the early 2000s, it ushered in the big data analytics era. Using Google's design innovation, Hadoop built an algorithm that could link hundreds of thousands of computers and get them to operate like one computer. Companies such as Yahoo and Facebook that had mountains of unstructured data could now find patterns and mine insights using Hadoop's open source system. They could see what users did on a page and customize their ads to increase conversion.

Key Takeaway: Moore's Law predicts advances in memory chips, as well.

Moore's Law applies not just to computational power, but to memory chips, as well. While a cellphone could not store a single photo a decade ago, the average phone today has 16 gigabytes of flash memory.

The inception of the cloud has especially been a game changer, enabling anyone with an internet connection to store and access data and software and perform virtually any computing task, anywhere.

Key Takeaway: Software and networking are reducing complexity.

Software reduces the complexity of sorting and retrieving information and solving problems. Application programming interfaces, or APIs, hide layers of operations in a computer or Web service so that you get instant solutions at the touch of a button.

Today, tools for writing software are improving exponentially, and platforms such as GitHub are fostering software development collaborations between individuals and organizations. These collaborations are helping create even more complex software to solve even more complex problems.

In large, advances in processing, storage, sensing and software have been made possible by advances in networking—which have also been accelerating at a pace close to Moore's law. Today, with fiber optics, computers on different continents can communicate at more than half the speed of light, transferring trillions of bits per second.

Key Takeaway: The cloud is fuelling technological capabilities, empowering individuals, groups, and institutions.

The cloud—a network of computer servers that offers computing capabilities, including data storage and access, to everyone, everywhere—is amplifying not just computing power, but human capabilities and idea flows, as well.

By merging advances in software and hardware, the cloud has negated the cost and accelerated the speed at which data can be digitalized, stored, accessed, analyzed, and distributed. Since problems are only complex because the information needed to solve them is either inaccessible or unintelligible, the cloud—and the sheer intelligence it packs—is negating the complexity of vast human problems.

"If you want to be a maker, a starter-upper, an inventor, or an innovator, this is your time. By leveraging the supernova (cloud) you can do so much more now with so little" (Kindle Locations 1614-1615).

The cloud has catalyzed the cognitive era of computing where computers are able to make sense of unstructured data and improve their analysis and prediction capabilities. Through the cloud, computers can be fed limitless examples of what is right and wrong to recognize patterns and learn. Artificial intelligence machines such as IBM's Watson are today harnessing the power of the cloud to access data, recognize patterns, and help doctors make diagnoses and find the best treatment options faster and more accurately.

Cloud apps are making virtually every industry computable, disrupting existing business models, and giving new ones the ability to scale globally overnight. Uber, for example, digitalized the taxi-hailing process, disrupted the industry, and democratized it so that anyone could be a cab driver or start a cab company. Airbnb set off the sharing economy and made an innkeeper out of anyone who wanted.

Key Takeaway: Globalization is interacting with technology to create limitless possibilities.

The explosion of globalization—the ability to connect, compete, and collaborate with anyone around the world—is facilitating interactions on an unprecedented scale, creating a flat, hyperconnected, and interdependent world. Through virtual interactions, people are sharing, more than ever before, ideas and innovations, empathy and truth, gossip and exclusion, education and finance.

The cloud is broadening participation in digital flows—be it software, music, opinions, photos, educational courses, or electronic payments—making virtually everyone the author of a global narrative. The global scale of online tools is easing cross-border interactions in such a way that anyone can start a business—on Facebook, Amazon, Alibaba, or on a personal website—that goes global from the first day.

Key Takeaway: Digital flows are driving business and microeconomic value.

Today, the value and security of a business is no longer in the knowledge or commodities it has in stock, it is the richness of the flows that pass through it and in its ability to leverage these flows. Any business that wishes to thrive in the modern marketplace has to make a constant presence in and participate in digital flows. It has to absorb and contribute to the new knowledge being created every day. Leading companies such as General Electronic no longer depend on their engineers to create the best designs; they supplement the knowledge of their engineers with the diverse inputs they get from the global contests they hold periodically.

Participation in global flows is vital because competition no longer comes from companies in the same industry or geography. It could come from anywhere. Amazon, which started out as an online retailer, now competes with cloud computing companies and Hollywood studios. What determines the prosperity of companies, industries, and even entire countries today is their level of openness to and participation in different types of global flows—including information, trade, finance, education, and culture.

Key Takeaway: The global socio-economic system is gradually pushing nature beyond the Holocene epoch.

In July 2015, the heat index rose to 163 degrees Farhrenheit in a city in the Middle East. This occurrence is only one of the recent extreme weather and climate readings that indicate the acceleration of global warming. Sea levels and concentrations of carbon dioxide are now higher than they have been in thousands of years, average global temperatures are on the rise, and Greenland is losing nearly 300 billion tons of ice per year. If these changes keep accelerating, humanity is at risk of losing the stable climatic conditions of the Holocene epoch that have made agriculture, civilizations, and modern life possible.

Since the 1950s, urban population, primary energy use, water use, fertilizer consumption, paper production, and foreign direction investments have increased exponentially. With technological advances and globalization empowering more people than ever before, humanity has become a force of nature, pushing current biophysical landscapes to the brink of a new state that cannot support life. Climate change, deforestation, mass biodiversity loss, and increased biogeochemical flows are already stretching the boundaries of a stable planetary system.

The United Nations projects that the global population in 2050 will be 9.7 billion, three times the global population in the 1950s. Some countries in West Africa, Asia, and the Middle East—where mortality rates are now low, fertility rates are high, and contraceptive use is stigmatized—will record as much as a 30-fold increase in population between 1950 and 2050, the consequence of which will be strained natural resources, political instability, and a global refugee crisis of an unmanageable scale.

Part of the solution to the looming planetary crisis is to encourage efficient energy consumption and put a hefty price tag on carbon to speed up large scale investments in clean energy. Part of the solution to the social crisis is to commit to women's education and empowerment, especially in countries with exploding populations.

PART III:
INNOVATING

Key Takeaway: Learn to adapt—it's the only way to survive the age of accelerations.

Although accelerations in the three forces are increasingly widening the gap between the rate of change and the rate of human adaptation, the only way through the fog is to learn to adapt. It's tempting to slow down or build walls, but the only way to navigate the change—as is the case with a kayaker moving through rough waters—is to increase momentum and move at or faster than the speed of the current.

Governments and entire societies have to reinvent geopolitics, workplaces, communities, and ethics to keep pace with technology, globalization, and climate change. The challenge is to get social technologies—the systems that govern, regulate, and foster learning and cooperation—to keep up with Moore's law and the physical technologies that follow its prediction.

Key Takeaway: The age of average, high-paid middle-skilled jobs, is over.

For decades after the Second World War, America dominated the global manufacturing industry and the world economy. With strong labor unions, few skills gaps, and limited outsourcing, workers with average skills could work average hours in average jobs and coast off to retirement with above-average savings.

In the age of accelerations, average doesn't cut it anymore. Technology and globalization keep lowering barriers to entry, multiplying disruptive events, and increasing performance pressure on both individuals and organizations. To get in the middle class, the contemporary worker has to make learning a continuous and lifelong process, constantly reinvent himself, and work harder than before.

Key Takeaway: The age of accelerations is ushering in a workplace that demands new social contracts.

Thriving in the new workplace and the new global economy demands four new social contracts:

1. Between the employee and his self. The individual will have to find the self-motivation to commit to lifelong learning.

2. Between employers & employees. Companies will have to keep updating requisite skills and offering learning opportunities.

3. Between educators and students. Schools will have to adapt curricula, teach new skills, and offer flexible courses—with on-demand mobility, reasonable tuition, and personalized speed.

4. Between governments and citizens. Legislation and economic policies will have to create incentives for organizations to offer mass learning and develop professional networks.

Technology, especially partial automation, is not doing away with jobs. It is creating new and more jobs but raising the skill and attitude requirements of workers. Part of increasing the adaptation rate is to lobby governments, social enterprises, and companies to use artificial intelligence to create platforms that offer lifelong learning, to improve interfaces and lessen the cognitive load so people can learn easily and faster, and to create networks to connect people to all skills and opportunities available.

Business executives need to paint a clear picture of where the organization is going, the challenges it will encounter, and the solutions or skills it will need. They need to create incentives for employees to take on continuous learning—including sponsoring courses, filling jobs internally first, and offering opportunities to employees who team with others and commit to learning. To survive the age of accelerations, employers will need to reskill the workforce and disrupt their companies' internal processes.

Schools need to set expiry dates on curriculums and bylaws, reinvent courses in response to technological innovations, and create new knowledge and new careers. Udacity, Coursera, and other providers of massive online courses offer a glimpse into the design of the new school.

In the age of accelerations, value is created by engaging people on a personal level. Schools need to emphasize social and cognitive skills because the occupations that cannot be automated are those that require softer skills such as cooperation, flexibility, and empathy. Since the 1980s, occupations that require a mix of technical knowhow and interpersonal skills have been consistently growing, both in numbers and wages.

Key Takeaway: Accelerations in the three forces are stressing states, threatening geopolitical stability.

Accelerations in technology, globalization, and climate change are triggering disorder in countries that can't handle the pressure. Climate change, for example, is killing agricultural productivity, and disgruntled individuals are leveraging technology to commit cybercrimes, join jihadists, organize illegal immigrations, and topple governments.

Disintegration of states to militarist groups—as is happening in Syria and Nigeria—is creating disorder, spilling refugees and economic migrants to other countries. America is increasingly being forced to step in to check the disorder before it spreads.

During the Cold War, America and the Soviet Union rebuilt, supported, and influenced their allies. The support of the superpowers kept disorder in check, even in countries that had average or below average leadership. Today, not America, Russia, or China can singlehandedly bear the burden of another country or impose order from outside—the bill is just too high. With no support, countries that were riding commodity booms are crumbling, and those that depended on agricultural production—especially in Africa and the Middle East—are struggling to stay intact. The Syrian crisis, for example, was sparked by Assad's failure to respond to the drought that started in 2006, one of the worst in modern history.

In countries where there's still order, accelerations have created economic interdependence and, consequently, blurred the line between ally and foe. Today, the political and economic actions of a nation like China or Russia have far-reaching consequences around the world. Checking the global influence of any one country is becoming an increasingly delicate balance.

Key Takeaway: Social media offers freedom from, not freedom to.

Recent revolutions such as the Arab Awakening have demonstrated that technology is effective in giving people the freedom *from*—from dictators, tyranny—but not the freedom *to*. It empowers individuals such that one person can use social media to tap into the fears of the masses and create a flash mob that topples a government. It's harder, in the wake of the revolution, to use the same platform to create the political culture, organization, and leadership that steers the country to political or economic freedom.

Even in the age of accelerations, creating order calls for the conventional approach of organizing physical meetings and engaging people on a personal level to create trust and desirable civic habits.

Key Takeaway: Technology empowers breakers as much as it empowers makers.

Technological accelerations have made it possible for anyone to source the right materials online, watch video tutorials, create improvised explosives, and cause any level of mass destruction imaginable. It has never been easier for people living on the margins of society to get radicalized.

Deterring breakers calls for a multi-faceted approach:

• Leverage community participation to check radicalism. Authorities have to encourage family and friends to identify and act on changes in behavior, and global watchdogs have to incentivize governments of countries with radical Islamism to declare war on rogue religious factions.

• Fund schools and universities to give young people the power to transform their countries.

• Offer opportunities—including building basic infrastructure, subsidizing basic farming inputs and training, and increasing accessibility to high-speed internet to connect the poor to global flows—so that the poorest peoples can remain in their homelands and stop emigrating.

• Deter the aggression of the other superpowers—China and Russia—while simultaneously enlisting their support in containing disorder in places like Syria and North Korea.

• Degrade terrorist groups such as ISIS using military power and local collaborations and incentivize local communities to delegitimize their agenda and oust their leaders.

"When the necessary is impossible but the impossible is necessary, when no power wants to own the World of Disorder but, increasingly, no power can ignore it, it is going to take these hybrid combinations of drones and walls, aircraft carriers and Peace Corps volunteers, plus chickens, gardens, and Webs, to begin to create stability in the age of accelerations" (Kindle Locations 5080-5082).

Key Takeaway: The ability to adapt determines the states and cultures that survive in the age of accelerations.

The internal politics of strong states—with their rigid bureaucracies and outdated agendas—cannot respond to current changes in technology, globalization, and the environment. The Republican Party, for example, cannot respond to climate change when it denies its existence, and the UK cannot address global immigration if its first move is to alienate itself from an organization that seeks solutions to the problem.

Rapid change demands radical thinking and political innovations. Given the accelerated rate of change, the most resilient states and cultures—the ones that advance the most—will be those who choose and learn to adapt to changing geopolitics. They will be the states and cultures that embrace diversity, take responsibility for their problems, nurture pluralism, balance internal systems (state and local governments, autonomous groups), and absorb new and foreign ideas, regardless of their source.

Societies that embrace pluralism in all its forms—in ideas, gender, and racial and ethnic groups—and open themselves to cultural diversity will have a wide base from which they can draw talent and innovations. Pluralism will be the new metric that measures which companies and countries thrive.

On the other hand, homogeneity will be the economic undoing of many states. Monocultures—the kind ISIS and Al Qaeda are attempting to create in Muslim-dominated countries—will close off societies to global innovations, breed dysfunctional ideas, and precipitate the death of entire societies.

Key Takeaway: Technological innovation must be accompanied by moral innovation.

Humanity is yet to grasp the consequences of the godlike power technology is giving every connected person. Owing to the gap between the launch of a new technology and mass understanding of its consequences, cyberspace is largely a free, lawless, valueless, and seemingly godless space. Moral innovations must accompany technological innovations to bridge this gap and limit the abuse of innovations.

When it comes to restraining immoral behavioral in the age of accelerations, laws, law enforcers, and informal morality codes are necessary but largely insufficient. What human societies need is a way to inspire values that nurture social bonds and generate trust and hope. One simple and adaptive solution is to emphasize the Golden Rule, which calls on people to do onto others only that which they would want done to them.

An effective moral innovation would be one that immerses people in strong, healthy communities. Communities create a sense of belonging. More than that, they create an environment that fosters trust, encourages people to do good, and delegitimizes destructive behaviors.

Key Takeaway: A healthy community is the bedrock of socio-economic prosperity.

Community institutions, including parks, schools, and sports and cultural centers, support not just the employability and productivity of their members, but their inclusion, as well. They are the first stops for the social innovations needed to navigate the age of accelerations.

St. Louis Park, Minnesota, where the author grew up in the 1950s, embodies the healthy community that thrives in the age of accelerations. Since the 1950s, the town had a liberal culture that welcomed Jews even when the larger Minneapolis was strongly anti-Semitic. Local politicians, who accepted divergent views and worked for the greater good, made decisions that supported the private sector. This environment encouraged leading businesses to give back to the community. They set up a club to which they donated—and still donate—5 percent of their profits to philanthropy.

Even today, St. Louis Park nurtures civic sensibilities in public schools, parks, and recreational facilities. It stresses politics as a vehicle towards the common good, not towards the common divide. Local leaders commit to develop spaces and experiences that mix classes and give everyone an opportunity to belong, connect, and collaborate. They understand that the pluralism that makes up a community is built on tolerance, respect, and trust.

Key Takeaway: Healthy communities are built on collaboration and compromise.

Part of what made St. Louis Park—and Minnesota, in extension—a successful community was its culture of compromise and collaboration. Leaders made compromises for the greater good, and the public sector collaborated with the private sector so that everyone took responsibility for the community. This combination created the trust that sustained positive habits in the community.

St. Louis Park still uses civic engagement to foster inclusion. It has neighborhood associations that the mayor consults to build consensus for key projects and others big decisions. The city gives these neighborhood associations grants to create neighborhood boards and hold community activities such as picnics.

The city has a council of business leaders, philanthropists, and school superintendents—all volunteers—who lobby for social progress and against retrogressive political divides. The council invites CEOs to confront unconscious biases and review hiring practices to close the racial achievement gap.

PART IV:
ANCHORING

Key Takeaway: Navigating the age of accelerations takes inclusion and adaptation.

America is turning up the dial on divisive politics at exactly the wrong time. What the country needs to do most of is build collaboration and trust to keep pace with accelerating innovations. It needs leaders who will make compromises and pursue the best practices, not minions who will only toe their party line.

The only way to take full advantage of accelerations in technology and globalization is to forge deep human connections and invest in social technologies. The best solutions for building resilience and successfully navigating the age of accelerations are not in the cloud; they are on the ground. Resilience will come from committing to lifelong learning and fostering human-to-human connections: from forging trust, taking ownership, nurturing community, and empowering communities ravaged by disorder to move towards civil decency.

Humanity has to anchor itself in community, because community makes all the difference; it spurs people to reach out, do things together, take risks, and share their growth.

EDITORIAL REVIEW

In his book *Thank You for Being Late*, Thomas L. Friedman argues that exponential accelerations in technology, globalization, and climate change are influencing every aspect of modern life—from the way people communicate and shop to the way schools and governments are run. He cautions that while the instinctive response to rapid change is to slow down or build walls, the people and institutions who successfully navigate these changes are those who keep moving and diving into the heart of the change. Friedman assures readers that as long as they keep reflecting on current change—as long as they keep learning, and adapting—everything will work out.

Through a series of interviews with people at the center of each of the three forces, Friedman offers a comprehensive overview of recent changes in technology, globalization, and the environment. He offers an elaborate explanation for why everything happening in the world today—from the Syrian crisis to the large-scale melting of ice caps in Greenland—feels like it's spinning out of control. The solution he offers is simple, perhaps too simple for all the overwhelming change he reviews. He calls on individuals, institutions, and entire societies to mimic nature—to be adaptable, to experiment, to discard everything that doesn't work, and to embrace diversity.

Friedman displays his journalistic mastery in his explanation of how everything is changing. His ability to bring together seemingly unrelated forces and show how they are interacting to change the world is sensational. His writing is only weakened by the lengthy personal narratives—which he weaves into the last pages of the book—that make no immediate contribution to his work.

ABOUT THE AUTHOR

Thomas L. Friedman is an American journalist and author. He writes a weekly column that covers foreign affairs, environmental issues, and global trade for *The New York Times*. Friedman, who is a three-time Pulitzer Prize winner, has authored several bestselling books including *The World is Flat* and *That Used to be Us*.

THE END

If you enjoyed this summary, please leave an honest review on Amazon.com…it'd mean a lot to us.

If you haven't already, we encourage you to purchase a copy of the original book.

Made in the USA
San Bernardino,
CA